Families and their Faiths

Sikhism in India

Written by Frances Hawker and Mohini Kaur Bhatia

Photography by Bruce Campbell

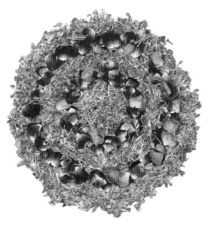

Tulip Books

TULIP BOOKS

www.tulipbooks.co.uk

This edition published by:
  Tulip Books
  Dept 302
  43 Owston Road
  Carcroft
  Doncaster
  DN6 8DA.

ISBN: 978-1-78388-017-1

Printed in Spain by Edelvives

Contents

My name is Pritam, but my grandchildren call me Dadiji. I live with my two sons and their families in a part of India called the Punjab.

I am going to tell you a story about Pulkit, one of my granddaughters. She is ten years old. Every morning we sit in the courtyard and her sister Survani and I plait her long hair.

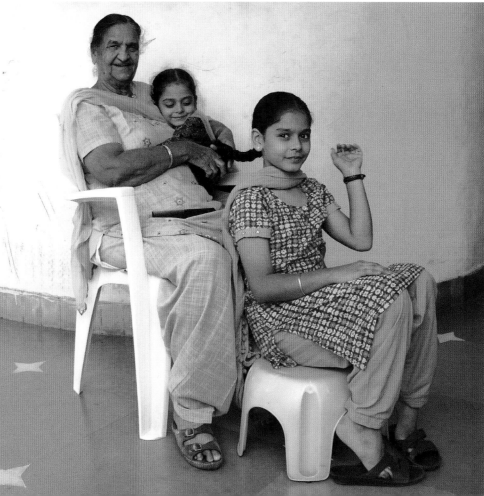

Sagarpreet, Pulkit's brother, also has long hair.
He ties it under his turban.

We are Sikhs, and no one in our family ever
cuts their hair. This shows that we are proud to
be Sikhs.

6

Each day we pray in our little prayer room. See the picture of Guru Nanak on the wall? He was our first guru. Guru means leader. Nine other gurus followed Guru Nanak. Now Sikhs think of our holy book as our guru or spiritual leader for all time.

We thank God for everything he has made. Pulkit is learning to meditate on God's name.

My grandchildren all play instruments. Pulkit is learning how to play drums called tabla. Her mother is teaching her little sister Survani how to play the harmonium.

They also sing hymns called kirtan. Next month they will sing kirtan at the Gurdwara, our place of worship.

Pulkit goes to school six days a week. She is taught in English but speaks Hindi and Punjabi with her friends.

After school she waves goodbye to her friends as she sets off home in a rickshaw.

On Sunday Pulkit does not have to go to school. We often visit Auntie and Uncle on their small farm. The children love visiting.

'Let's see if we can find some flowers to make garlands, Dadiji!' Pulkit calls to me. Garlands are offerings to God.

After collecting flowers, Pulkit helps Auntie
Malkeet make tea with milk from Uncle's cow.

Finally it's time to leave.

'Come on, Dadiji,' everyone calls to me.
'Let's go to the market. There are plenty of
flowers there.'

On the way home we stop and buy marigolds
and rose petals to decorate the Gurdwara and
make garlands.

The celebration of Guru Nanak's birthday starts on Monday. Guru Nanak started our religion nearly 500 years ago.

After school, Pulkit and Survani help me make garlands with the flowers that we bought yesterday.

When I go upstairs to hang out the washing on the roof, I look down and see the beautiful design Pulkit and Survani are making with flower petals.

Quick! We rush outside to watch the parade go by.

Mother gives some of our garlands to the boys who lead the parade. They remind us of the Five Beloved Ones. These were the first five men who joined the Khalsa, the Sikh community.

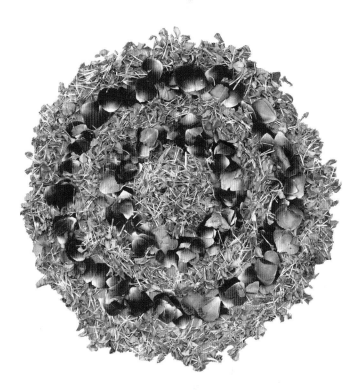

We watch as the streets are washed and rose petals thrown on the ground. The Guru Granth Sahib, our holy book, is carried on a float. We treat it very carefully: it sits on a cushion. It is a collection of verses and hymns given to us by God.

The men on the front of the float hand out a special sweet called prasad. Pulkit's mother gives them our flower garlands. She comes back with two balls of prasad that have been blessed.

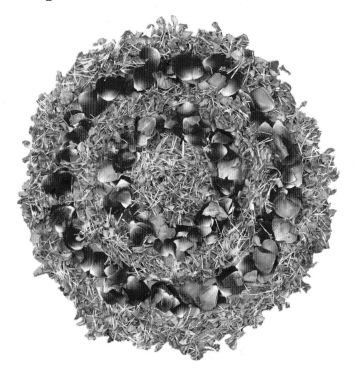

Tomorrow is Guru Nanak's actual birthday. The children will have the day off school. Our Gurdwara will offer free food called Langar to everyone.

But first there is lots of work to be done! Sacks of potatoes, onions and cauliflowers need to be washed and chopped. Everyone helps. It is an important part of our religion to help others. This is called seva.

The next day, people are up before dawn to cook for the Langar. Huge pots of food are cooked over open fires in the street behind our Gurdwara. Pulkit stirs one of the pots.

Inside, women and children are busy making thousands of flat pieces of bread called chapatis.

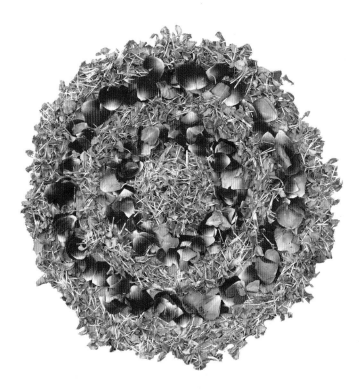

We go into the Gurdwara to listen to hymns from the Guru Granth Sahib. We must cover our heads and wash our feet before we enter the room.

We bow down and touch the floor with our foreheads in front of the Guru Granth Sahib, then kneel and say a short prayer. Three musicians sing and play hymns from the holy book.

Singing prayers brings us closer to God. The prayers tell us how to lead our lives.

After visiting the Gurdwara we are always given prasad, the wonderful sweet that has been blessed. See Survani holding a bowl made of leaves pressed together. Isn't that a clever way to make a bowl?

Pulkit and Sagarpreet help serve the food at the Langar. People from every religion are welcome. The rich and poor sit next to each other on the ground. Everyone is equal in front of God. It is chance for very poor people to have a good meal.

The children stay up very late. After visiting the Gurdwara again we come home and light candles around the house to celebrate Guru Nanak's birthday. Everywhere in the city, families are lighting fireworks.

Finally Pulkit falls asleep on my lap. She has worn herself out doing the things Guru Nanak asks us to do: praying, working, sharing and doing seva.

I whisper to her, 'You are a True Sikh.'

Notes for Parents and Teachers

Sikhism is the youngest of the six religions featured in this series of books and was founded 500 years ago by Guru Nanak. Guru Nanak was born in the small town of Talwindi, near Lahore, which is now part of Pakistan. He was raised as a Hindu, but as a young man he began developing ideas of his own for a new religion.

There are over 20 million Sikhs in the world today, mostly living in the Punjab. Sikhs believe in one God who is everywhere in the world, and who does not have human form.

Sikhs follow the teachings of the ten Gurus and the Guru Granth Sahib, the eternal Sikh book of holy scripture. They believe that everyone has equal access to God and that all people are equal before God.

Page 5

Fully observant Sikhs, both men and women, never cut their hair. Men keep their hair coiled up and covered by a turban, and never shave, and women usually wear long plaits. The keeping of hair in its natural state is regarded as living in harmony with the will of God, and is a symbol of being a member of the Sikh faith and community.

Page 6

Guru Nanak was the first Sikh guru. He established the system of guruship, and was followed by nine other gurus. The tenth guru, Guru Gobind Singh, died in 1708 and did not name another guru to follow him. Instead, he told the Sikhs that they should follow the Guru Granth Sahib (see notes to pages 18 and 19).

Page 8

A Gurdwara is a building where Sikhs come together to worship. Gurdwara means 'residence of the guru'. A Gurdwara is not just a place of worship, but also a place for teaching Sikh traditions to children and a community centre. It has a communal kitchen for Langar. Gurdwaras have four doors to signify that they are open to all people, not just Sikhs. The Golden Temple at Amritsar is the holiest Gurdwara for Sikhs from all over the world.

A formal ceremony in the Gurdwara consists of singing hymns, chanting, meditating on the name of God, praying and a short lesson. Sometimes Sikhs simply bow down before the Guru Granth Sahib, pray and then leave. Pulkit does this every morning before going to school.

Pages 16 and 17

The tenth guru, Guru Gobind Singh, introduced a new initiation ceremony for Sikhs in 1699, and five volunteers now called 'the Five Beloved Ones' became the first members of the Khalsa or new Sikh community. Khalsa members from that time on have been required to wear the five emblems of the Khalsa, called the Five Ks:

- Kesh - unshorn hair and beard
- Kanga - a wooden comb in the hair to keep it tidy
- Kara - a steel bracelet
- Kaccha - short breeches worn as underwear
- Kirpan - a knife or sword. Because Sikhs were often persecuted in the past they carry a knife as a symbol that they are ready to defend their religion and the weak and oppressed.

Pages 18 and 19

The Guru Granth Sahib is the only Sikh book of holy scriptures. Most of it was written by the Sikh gurus but a few poems by holy Hindu and Muslim writers are also included. The tenth guru, Guru Gobind Singh, decreed that after his death there would be no more human gurus. Sikhs would instead take the Guru Granth Sahib as their eternal guru and source of religious teachings.

Page 20

Sikhs do not believe that people should devote themselves only to their religion. A good life is one that is lived as part of the community, and Sikhs should strive to live and work honestly, care for others and perform community service or seva.

Pages 22 to 24

Langar is the name of both the kitchen attached to the Gurdwara and the communal meal that is served free of charge to anyone who comes to the Gurdwara. The food served is always vegetarian to ensure that it is suitable for any visitor, even visitors of other faiths who may have dietary restrictions. The tradition of Langar was started by Guru Nanak. Everyone sits together on the ground as equals, regardless of their wealth or status, religion or caste. Men and women sit together. The food is provided, prepared and served by members of the Sikh community and children usually help in the preparation and serving of the food. Assistance with the provision of Langar is an important part of the tradition of seva or community service that Sikhs are expected to participate in.

Glossary

Chapatis	Flat round pieces of bread
Courtyard	An outside area
Garland	A string of flowers
Gurdwara	The place where Sikhs gather to worship
Guru	Special people chosen to give God's message to the world
Guru Granth Sahib	The Sikh holy book. It is their eternal guru
Guru Nanak	The founder of Sikhism and the first guru
Harmonium	A keyboard instrument
Hindi	The main language spoken in northern India
Khalsa	The family or community of Sikhs who wear the Five Ks
Kirtan	Singing hymns from the Guru Granth Sahib
Langar	The kitchen, and the meal Sikhs provide after worship
Marigold	A kind of flower
Meditate	To concentrate deeply on something
Prasad	Holy sweet made from sugar, flour and ghee
Punjabi	The language of the region called the Punjab
Rickshaw	A three-wheeled bicycle with room for passengers
Seva	Community service
Turban	A length of material that is wound around the head

Index